KEN MARKELL

THE TALENT CODE

The Ultimate Guide to Talented Kids Secrets, Discover the
Best Practices and Methods on How to Discover the
Talent and Bring The Best Out of Your Child

Descrierea CIP a Bibliotecii Naţionale a României
KEN MARKELL
    THE TALENT CODE. The Ultimate Guide to Talented
Kids Secrets, Discover the Best Practices and Methods on How
to Discover the Talent and Bring The Best Out of Your Child /
Ken Markell – Bucharest: Editura My Ebook, 2020
    ISBN

KEN MARKELL

THE TALENT CODE

The Ultimate Guide to Talented Kids Secrets, Discover the Best Practices and Methods on How to Discover the Talent and Bring The Best Out of Your Child

My Ebook Publishing House
Bucharest, 2020

CONTENTS

INTRODUCTION

Have you ever had the thought that your child was brilliant? Every parent has thought this at some point or another. As our children grow from toddlers and begin learning very quickly, it amazes us at how fast they progress. But are they truly talented?

The fact of the matter is that every child is talented. Every child fills us with wonder as they learn and grow. Your child can easily become a smart, gifted and talented child. The difference between children considered to be talented and those who are not is simple. Talented children have been encouraged and groomed to be so.

Bringing out the best in your child is actually pretty easy to do. It takes some time and dedication. Most parents are already dedicated to spending a lot of time with their child, so this is an easy requirement to fulfill. Talking with your child candidly and allowing them to ask questions is the best way to help them grow into talented children.

The following chapters will help you understand how to interact with your child to encourage them and develop their mind. You will be able to take everything you learn here and apply it to your child's daily life. As you continue on this path, you will notice that your child is truly talented. The road to success as a child and later in life is easy as pie once you have reached that point.

CHAPTER 1

HOW TO ENCOURAGE KIDS
TO EXPRESS THEIR FEELINGS

Children should be encouraged to express their feelings. This should start at an early age, usually as a toddler. There are several reasons that this is important.

Children should be comfortable openly expressing their feelings. Being given this ability gives the child a certain amount of freedom. If a child is not comfortable talking about their feelings, they are also less likely to speak up when they have an idea or a creative moment. Encouraging a child to express their feelings also helps them be encouraged to share thoughts, dreams and goals as they get older.

Expressing one's feelings is also an important part of the creative process. Breeding creativity can be difficult with some children. By encouraging them to openly express their feelings, they can more actively access those feelings and thoughts and turn them into creative genius.

Another advantage of this is that they will develop a huge sense of self confidence. As they recognize, own and express their feelings they will feel very confident in their abilities and their place in the world. This is a major trait of every successful and talented child.

There are many ways to teach your child to express their feelings. The methods you use should coincide with the age of the child. In addition, it is important that you continue to encourage your child to express their feelings as they get older. Here are some of the ways you can teach your child how to express their feelings.

Prompting

The most important thing you can do is ask them how they feel about different situations that come up daily. Ask them what they are feeling and help them put it into words. Ask their opinion about small decisions, such as what is for lunch.

Ask them why they have that opinion and encourage them to share their feelings and ideas with you. Pure conversation is the best way to encourage openness.

Teaching Toddlers

Toddlers are just beginning to learn how to express themselves. They have feelings about everything but are unable to express them. It is your job to teach them the words for all of the feelings that they have.

Do's and Don't's

Many parents go about this by asking the child if they are feeling a certain way. If another child takes their toy, the parent may ask, "Are you feeling angry?" This is not the best way to name feelings. Your child may not be angry at all, but be sad instead. Since they do not know the names for their feelings, being prompted in this way may make them misunderstand what feelings are expressed by which word.

Instead, you should give your child names for feelings in a neutral setting. At a time of play, tell your child that you feel happy. When it's time for bed tell your child that you feel sleepy. By expressing your own feelings in daily situations, your child will begin to understand what words go with which feelings.

It is also important that you help your children learn the right and wrong way to express emotions. If they get angry and hit someone, talk to them about another way they could have dealt with the emotion that wouldn't have hurt someone.

Giving your child guidance and options in the moment and after the fact will help them learn to express their emotions in productive and peaceful ways.

You should also praise your child for expressing their feelings. Don't just react to their process, but let them know that it is a good thing that they expressed their feelings in whatever way they are comfortable with. Even if they express them in a negative way, praise them for letting people know how they feel while also explaining that another method would have been better. This will encourage your child to continue expressing their feelings on a daily basis.

Teaching with Pictures

Another way that you can teach your child about feelings is through pictures. Cut a strip of poster board and draw a face for each feeling. Start with the basics: happy, sad, angry and sleepy.

As your child learns and grows you can add faces to the strip: frustrated, confused, interested and creative are some examples.

Write the feeling beneath the face. Even though your child cannot read yet, you can continue to use this tool as they become older, until they fully understand the scope of their feelings.

Post a copy of this strip in each room your child spends time in. When something happens throughout the day, ask your child to point to the face that shows how they are feeling. If they point to the happy face, for example, point to it and say, "That means happy. Are you happy?" In this way you are giving your child the opportunity to express themselves and learn the names for their feelings without being prompted.

Learning Through Stories

You can also teach your child about feelings as part of daily play and learning. Read them stories about feelings, or make your own picture book. "The dog licks Sally's face. Sally is happy." Or "Jack took the toy away. Sam is sad." These types of stories will help your child begin to associate words with their feelings, and help them understand what feelings are.

Make an Emotion Book

This teaching tool combines artwork and storytelling. It is appropriate for toddlers who are already able to hold a decent conversation. Staple some pages together to make a book. Draw a face showing an emotion, such as a smiley face. Write happy under the face. Then, ask your child to fill the book with things that make them happy. You can make one book for each emotion.

The Emoticon Memory Game

Making games for learning about feelings is also easy to do. You can purchase these types of games from a number of online stores that sell teaching tools.

However, making your own game can be very fun for you, and fun and interesting for your child. A memory game is a perfect way for your child to develop retention skills while also learning about feelings. A picture could be matched up with an emoticon for each pair, and the most pairs wins. For example, a shiny new toy could be paired with a smiley face.

Encouraging Young Children

As children move out of toddlerhood it may seem that they are a bit more detached. Children of this age are learning more about themselves and the world around them. They are able to communicate effectively, most of the time, to tell you their wants and needs. At the same time they are too busy with playing and learning to spend much time just sitting and talking to you.

It is important that you let your child know that they can always come to you if they need you. Even if they just need to talk to someone about their feelings they should feel comfortable seeking you out. At this point they should be able to express their feelings appropriately when prompted to do so. However, the key now is to get them to express feelings without prompting.

In addition, your child at this age should begin expressing their feelings to others. They should feel comfortable telling a friend or sibling that they are angry. They should be able to express that they are sad or upset without crying about every little thing. However, crying should still be treated with respect, as this is an important outlet that should not be discouraged.

The best way to get your child to openly express their feelings without prompting is to always listen to them. If you truly listen to your child and attempt to make conversation with them you will quickly discover how expressive your child can be. While it can be tedious to try to have a conversation with a four year old, the benefits you and your child reap from the experience will be well worth the effort.

Elementary Children

At this age your child is perfectly able to express their feelings. It is now time to encourage them to do so in new ways. Instead of simply stating their feelings at the time, they should learn to analyze their feelings and use the experiences to better themselves.

It is helpful for children of this age, boys and girls, to begin keeping a journal. They can record their feelings and experiences for each day, and then look back on them later. This will help them look at their feelings objectively and also start to notice the patterns of their behavior. They will also be encouraged through this process to analyze the feelings of others.

The journal is only the first step to helping your child express their feelings in a tangible format. You should encourage your child to write their feelings in the form of poetry or stories. This will often stem naturally from the journal writing.

You can also encourage your child to use art to express their feelings. They can sketch doodles or paint a masterpiece, it is entirely up to them. Giving them the option for this outlet is all you really need to do. Explain to them that this is one way to express feelings and that it can help to let them out. Make sure they have all of the materials they might need for painting, sketching, watercolors, or chalks. Get them whatever art materials they ask for, and let their imaginations and feelings run wild.

Wrapping Up

It is through creative outlets that feelings are best expressed. It is also through these mediums that your child will begin to show you how talented they are. Even if they are not destined to be a famous author or artist, these are just the beginning. Creative outlets are everywhere, and feelings can be harnessed and used to pursue any talent, mundane or creative.

The more you encourage these types of outlets and expressions of your child's feelings, the more comfortable they will be with themselves and others. They will also grow to be more outgoing and confident in themselves, which is a key characteristic of any talented child.

CHAPTER 2

DON'T OVERLOAD LEARNING PROCESS

Teaching your child to express their feelings is just one of the many things that you must teach them in order to develop them into a talented kid. There are many things that children learn during the early development years. It is your job to make sure that they learn everything they need to know, and if possible work ahead to give them a head start in school and in life.

However, it is important that you do not overload them in the process. Children can easily become overwhelmed. If that happens you will be facing an uphill battle. It can become difficult to get them to retain information, and they may take a step backward. These are just some of the ways that overloading your child with information can have a negative impact.

Negative Impact

Children who are overwhelmed with information cannot retain it. Particularly children ages 2-5 must be given ample time to absorb the information and apply it. When you give them too much information on too many topics in a short period of time, chances are that they will not remember any of the information you give them. Worse, they could easily become confused and get the wrong idea. You have to give your kids some breathing room.

Overloading the learning process can also make your child dread learning activities. It is no longer fun, but a chore that they don't want to do. This attitude will often carry on to the rest of their education and their adult lives. You need to make learning fun and engaging for it to be effective in developing a talented kid.

When children become overloaded and feel overwhelmed they may also act out. In a Texas study of fourth graders that asked how children felt when overloaded, most of them responded with words like angry, frustrated, mad, or furious. This makes it easier to understand why children who are overloaded with information act out in learning situations. Your child cannot learn and become talented if they are unwilling to learn, or unable to learn because of their attitude toward learning.

On the other hand, if your child feels fear or anxiety about learning they can also have trouble advancing. Fear about learning comes from a need to get every answer right. They are afraid of letting you down and answering a question wrong, or being unable to understand the concept right away. Anxiety about learning generally comes from the feeling that learning is difficult, and that the child feels easily confused. Both of these problems can be overcome if recognized by the parent or teacher.

Signs of an Overloaded Child

You will easily be able to tell if your child is feeling overwhelmed by their behavior. Knowing what to look for is half the battle. If your child exhibits any of these behaviors you should seriously consider cutting back on anything that might be causing them stress, including excessive learning.

Headaches or Illness, Real or Fake

You should take note if your child begins routinely complaining of headache or stomach cramps. Your child may be getting headaches due to stress. Stomach cramps can also be a sign of severe stress. If your child only seems to get these headaches when it is time to learn it very well may be a ruse. However, this is still a sign that your child is so overwhelmed or overloaded on learning that they no longer which to participate.

Restlessness and Agitation

If your child is generally calm but begins to show signs of restlessness they are likely suffering from overload. This is especially true if the restlessness happens just before, during, or just after learning activities. They may fidget or have trouble sitting still. They may even be unable to sit for very long, and continuously get up from their chair and wander around.

Irritability and Negative Attitude

If your child is generally easy going, but suddenly develops a negative attitude, they may be suffering from overload. They may also become very irritable, with every little thing making them upset or angry. These behaviors may occur all day, or just around the time of learning activities.

Disinterest

If your child is usually willing to learn and enjoys learning activities, but suddenly loses interest, they are probably overloaded. This is especially true of fun activities such as painting, coloring, or interactive learning with games or computers. If these things do not interest your child and they do not seem to be enjoying them any longer, you are probably using them too frequently.

Dependency

Sometimes when a child is overloaded they will begin to refuse to do things for themselves. If your child suddenly comes to depend on you more than usual, or asks you to do things for them you know they can do themselves, it is time to evaluate what might be stressing your child. It may be time to cut back on lessons, or introduce some new activities that might be more fun.

Antisocial Behavior

In extreme cases overload can result in antisocial behavior. Your child may suddenly become withdrawn and unwilling to play with others. They may even start lying often, or even try to steal. Any antisocial behavior should be addressed immediately, and you should do whatever you can to alleviate the stress causing it before it spirals out of control.

Do's of Learning

There a lot of ways that you can teach your child everything you want them to learn without overloading them in the process. It is important that you recognize warning signs and work to actively address them early, before a general attitude about learning can develop. Use this list to help you keep your child from becoming overloaded.

Take Breaks

It is important that you give your child time to play. Taking breaks only for meals or important activities will not give your child any real down time. While you can take advantage of situations that come up in play or daily to teach a small lesson, it is important that this play time is not overloaded with learning. It should still feel like play time. Give your child plenty of time to pursue their own interests. This will not only give them a break from active learning, but it could also give you insight into what talents and capabilities your child will have as they grow and develop.

Never Push

If your child is restless and cannot sit still, you need to lighten up on the learning activities and give them a chance to work it out. Instead of forcing your child to sit back down and trying to make them pay attention, let them get up and walk around a bit. You might even send them into the backyard to run the length of the fence to get some energy out. They will feel much better afterward and may be more willing to sit down to the learning activities you had planned.

One Topic at a Time

You should never address more than one topic at a time, particularly with children ages 2-5. Addressing multiple topics may make them confused, and they will be unable to grasp any of the concepts. You will need to make sure that they fully understand one topic before moving on to the next.

Few Lessons per Day

Toddlers should have only two or three lessons per day. You can supplement this learning with teaching opportunities during play or routine daily activities. For example, one day you may work on shapes and the alphabet, and the next you may work on counting and colors. You can reinforce these lessons by asking your child what color their toy is while they are playing, or by asking them what shape the wheels are on the car next to you while driving through town.

Children ages four to five can have a few more lessons per day. You can begin teaching them how to write the alphabet and numbers, what sounds the alphabet makes, and begin teaching them how to read. You can probably provide your child with structured learning four or five times per day. Many talented kids begin learning these things at around three years of age. This is fine as well as long as you do not try to do too many lessons in one day.

Short Lesson Periods

It is important that you do not try to force your child to stay at their lessons for long periods of time. Young children do not have very long attention spans. If you go on too long they will become fidgety and start to refuse to participate. This will lessen the effect of what you are trying to accomplish.

You should not try learning activities longer than 20-30 minutes for toddlers. For younger children you can go a bit longer, 45-60 minutes. If you choose to go as long as an hour for each learning session, you should probably limit them to no more than three per day to give them plenty of down time.

Be Specific

Make sure that you are very specific with your instruction. You should make each lesson tailored to your child's strengths and abilities. Make sure that everything you do is age appropriate. You will find that your child grasps concepts better if you teach them a little bit at a time. You can always expand on the topic at a later time if they seem ready and willing to tackle the task.

Take Your Time

You will need to take your time when teaching your child. Young children often do not grasp concepts immediately. Even if they are very talented and pick up on things right away, that doesn't mean that they are going to retain the information. Explain to your child what you are trying to teach them. Ask them questions and give them the chance to do the same. Play a game or do another activity that will reinforce the concept and help them retain it. You will also want to address the topic on another day to make sure that they remember the information. Don't rush the process.

Make Learning Fun

Your child will enjoy learning and not become overloaded if they find learning fun. Use games, stories, and other tools to make learning enjoyable. The more fun your child has learning, the more they will go on to actively pursue additional learning. In addition, children who have fun while learning associate the lesson with a positive experience, helping them to retain the information.

Relate Learning to Everyday Life

When children are able to apply what they have learned to everyday situations, it keeps them from being overwhelmed with information. Teaching your child through daily experiences is the best way to do this. Even if you are sitting down with your child for an active learning session you should help them apply what they are learning to something that they are familiar with. When they understand why they are learning the concept they are much more likely to enjoy the lesson and retain the information.

What to Do When Your Child is Overloaded

Even if you do your best, you may find that your child is on information overload. There are several things you can do to alleviate this problem so that you can move forward in their education. If you follow these simple steps your child will be back to normal in no time. You can then use the tools above to ensure that it doesn't happen again.

Accent the Positive

Focus your child's attention on the gains they have made, rather than on the education itself. Give your child plenty of rewards for what they have learned, and help them understand that this will benefit them greatly in the future. You will probably want to take a break from active learning activities, but you can still encourage them in their endeavors by offering them play time and time for art projects and reading, which will reinforce learning without pressure. They will realize through these activities how much they have learned, and focus on that positive aspect.

Schedule Family and Free Time

You need to schedule time to spend as a family. Children who are overloaded often benefit from additional family time. This allows them time to be themselves and enjoy some closeness with those they love and are familiar with. It is time spent in fun activities with no pressure. While the child will not be the center of attention, they will be getting the attention that they need the most.

Shoot for Balance

Many parents are so determined to have talented kids that they aim for perfection. They want their child to be the smartest, the most talented, and the best at everything. The problem with this is that kids just need to be kids. If you focus on perfection, you will not be allowing your child the freedom to just act like a kid. There has to be balance. Make sure that your child is able to be themselves and play even while learning.

Start or Join a Play Group

Children need time with others their own age. Especially when a child is overloaded they need time with their peers. This also allows them to be just a kid, around other kids that are just being themselves. Regular play group time will benefit your child greatly. When things are back to normal the play group will give them something to look forward to, and help keep them from being overloaded in the future.

Wrapping Up

When your child shows from an early age that they are a talented kid, it is easy to get caught up in trying to push them to realize their potential. But if you push them too hard, you will not make any progress. In fact, you may actually overload them and cause them to take steps backward. Keep this in mind as you encourage your child to develop, and as you work to recognize their strengths and turn them into talents.

CHAPTER 3

HOW TO FOCUS ON STRENGTHS TO TALENTS

Every child has a talent. The trick is to discover what it is at a young age so that talent can be developed. In order to find your child's talent, you need to pay close attention to their strengths. It is also important to provide plenty of opportunities to try new things.

If you pay close attention to your child you will begin to see their strengths early on. Your child may like music, sing, dance, act out stories, tell stories, or like to paint or sculpt. Any of these behaviors can be developed into more than one talent.

Many children have multiple talents. Truly talented kids can learn multiple skills in a given area very easily. For example, if your child loves music, they may easily develop talents in singing as well as playing the piano or another instrument. A child who is into gymnastics may also excel at dance. A child who likes to paint could easily become talented in sketching, sculpture, and other art forms.

You will never know what your child can do until you let them try. Exposure to multiple talents over the course of their development years will help children discover their interests, while also allowing you to determine what talents are likely to develop. From there you can go on to work with your child to develop strengths into talents that will serve them well for the rest of their lives.

Toddlers

Toddlers stay very busy exploring their world. This is your greatest opportunity to expose your child to basic experiences in a wide variety of talent areas. Take this time to offer your child opportunities to show their strengths and try out new activities. Make the experiences fun and encourage a sense of adventure in your child as they experiment with these new concepts and abilities.

Art

Creative experiences include anything that encourages your child to make something new. Try art experiences like finger painting, coloring, sketching with regular or colored pencils, making collages or modeling with salt-based dough. In addition to pre-made coloring books, you can also print off coloring sheets from online sources or encourage your child to color in a sketch they have made.

Collages are easy to make: just cut out pictures from a magazine and give them to your child along with washable glue and a paper to glue them on so they can create their own collage designs. You can easily find recipes for salt-based modeling dough online and make it yourself.

Be aware that your child might not know what to do with these art media at first. The best way to help them explore is to sit down and do your own project right along beside them. They will see how you do it, get ideas of their own, and add their own special twist to it. Remember to praise the effort even if you do not find it attractive. After all, your child is just learning what the creative process is. Also, your child's artistic style might not appeal to you, but it is their own individual expression. The same is true of every artist whether child or adult. Just because you are not immediately drawn to your child's artwork, it does not mean that others will not like it.

Parents commonly post their child's artwork around the house, either on the refrigerator or on a wall. This tends to become annoying after awhile. Your child might be producing several pieces of toddler-style art every day, and once you start posting it in a prominent place, your child comes to expect it.

A better solution is to get a nice box and decorate it. Then, store all the artworks except one. Let your toddler choose which one to display, and then store away the others in the box. Get the box out once a week to look at all the projects your toddler has completed. Point out what you like about your child's creations and encourage your child to talk about what they thought about while making it or now that they see it again. Get out the box when grandparents or other relatives come to visit and ask your child if they would like to show their art to their grandma and grandpa. If they say no, don't push them to do it anyway.

Music

Toy xylophones are great fun, but too many parents limit their children's music experiments to only that one toy. You can make musical instruments from materials you have around your house. Percussion instruments are the easiest to make. All you need is some kind of container and some dry beans to place inside. Secure the lid to the container and show your child the sound of the shaker instrument. Turn on some music and shake the instrument in time to the beat of the music. Then, hand the shaker to your child and let them go wild.

You can also buy children's musical instruments in some specialty stores and online. Choose from shakers, wooden drums, rhythm sticks, melody harps, thumb pianos, whistles, chimes, slide whistles, harmonicas, jingle bells and tambourines, to name only a few. Do not force your child to use them. Simply use them yourself once to show them how it works. Then, store the items in the child's playroom or wherever they can find them if they want to use them. At this age, enthusiasm and joy are much more important than having perfect rhythm or tone quality.

Exposure to music is especially important during toddlerhood. Children's music helps spark your child's interest in music because it is generally upbeat and usually has fun lyrics. However, do not rely exclusively on children's songs as your child's introduction to music. Listen to the music you like when your toddler is with you, but also play a variety of other music genres. Sing when you get the urge. Dance when the notion strikes you. Enjoy your toddler's pleasure in the music.

Your toddler is happier when you respond enthusiastically to their activities. Always make listening to music as positive an experience as possible. Even if you listen to a sad song, you have an opportunity to talk to your child about how the song helps you express your feelings.

Even toddlers can begin playing the piano. At first, let your child experiment with the sounds they can make on the piano. Left unattended, a child usually bangs on the keys and may damage your piano. Instead, sit on the bench beside them and encourage them to touch the keys more softly. Later, you can begin teaching simple songs like "Mary Had a Little Lamb" or "Chopsticks."

As they improve their skills, teach them to play more complex songs, and then to read music. If you do not know how to play the piano, get your child into piano lessons. Your child's readiness is important in deciding when to start music lessons. The child should be showing consistent interest and patience in learning. At the same time, if you wait too long to start, the interest can die and your child can miss the opportunity to develop this skill.

Acting

Acting is embracing the spirit of make believe and imitation. Give toddlers used clothing, shoes and hats to play dress-up. Get dress-up items for different careers such as police officer hats, hard hats, chef hats, firefighter outfits and sports pads and jerseys. Allow them to play house, and encourage them to choose both traditional and nontraditional roles.

You can develop their acting skills further by explaining that a part of acting is recreating actions and emotions from real life. Have them watch themselves in the mirror as they brush their teeth or make silly faces. Then when they are with you in another room, tell them to show you how they do that activity.

Elementary children are ready to participate in theater groups. If they show interest and aptitude for acting, take the time to get them to practices and performances. Ask the child's theater director for tips on practicing acting skills for the production at home. Get an extra play book and read parts with them.

Then, go to the performances with them and enjoy the show. Let your child see that they made you proud and happy by performing well, but do not point out mistakes. Your child is probably already well aware of them, and overemphasis on failures is not a productive way to develop your child's strengths into talent.

Storytelling

Some children just love to tell stories. They have vivid imaginations and come up with interesting and often funny stories to tell you. These children often become the storytellers of the world. They grow up to be authors, poets, playwrights, screenwriters and lyricists. And they are never too young to get started creating interesting storylines.

Listen to your child's idle ramblings and notice elements of imaginative thinking. Many parents discourage their toddlers from talking about things that they, as parents, do not see as real. However, your toddler's world is very different from yours. They have a different reality. In their world, everything is new. They haven't formed the same biases and opinions as you have. Even when you feel that they are lying to you, notice the imaginative qualities of what you see as a lie. You don't have to condone bad behavior, but you can indeed acknowledge this form of creativity by interacting imaginatively with your child at another time.

One way to help your toddler develop storytelling skills is to start a story yourself and give your child the chance to finish it. Don't pressure them. Instead, ask them to participate by saying, "What do you think would happen next?" If the child doesn't chime in, just finish the story yourself so they don't feel like they have let you down. Keep it fun and keep it casual.

Building

Some toddlers enjoy building with simple toddler stacking or snap-together building blocks. Certain toddlers get interested in blocks as soon as they can manipulate them. Others develop the desire to build things later on. If you see your child stacking up toys, crackers or anything else in their environment, they might have an untapped potential to become great builders as they grow up.

Start encouraging them to develop this skill by having one set of building blocks in a location where they can sue it on their own. Later, you can add to this one set, or provide a completely different set of building materials.

Dance and Sports

Help your child explore their physical strengths by giving them ample opportunities to get up and move around. Dance to music and clap when your toddler dances with you.. Do physical movements with your child as you listen to music. Some old favorites are "The Hokey Pokey" and "The Wheels on the Bus

Go Round and Round." Try these or make up your own special movements that go with songs your toddler enjoys.

Go outdoors in your backyard or in the park if the weather is nice. Play with big rubber balls by kicking them, throwing them and rolling them across the yard. Get a plastic t-ball set and pitch as your older toddler hits the ball and runs the bases. Play tag, or just run around the yard. Sign your child up for toddler swim classes or water play groups. Get up and move with your child instead of sitting down and watching them. You will not only be healthy, but you will also be a role model for being fit and active.

Toddlers are already old enough to sign up for gymnastics and dance classes. If you notice your child doing somersaults or dancing to music, sign them up for a class. Then, act as their biggest supporter. Rather than demanding achievement, cheer your child on from the audience. Let the group leader set expectations and choose exercises. Right now, your child just needs to discover and enjoy.

Achievement can come later if your child is interested and has the strength and coordination to do the activity.

Math

Toddlers obviously can't do complicated math problems, or at least only a few rare children can do them. However, you can introduce your child to math concepts in a fun way. Count things with them as a game. For instance, you can count trucks on the highway as you take a long drive or count grapes as they pop them into their mouths. Give them shape-sorter toys to discover geometry basics. Toddler puzzles also help your child recognize shapes and sizes. Introduce them to the concept of distance by counting steps. Toddlers can begin learning about time by having a regular schedule.

Elementary Children

By the time children are in elementary school, they have already been exposed to many areas of talent. They have had music and art classes in school and have participated in group physical activities. Now is the time to focus on developing skills beyond simple exploration.

Continue to do fun activities at home after school and during vacations. Show your joy in learning and developing new skills of your own. Your child learns that this is an important and happy part of life. At the same time, do not make a point of being stronger or more talented than your child. Of course you are stronger!

And you have had many more years to develop your talents. Show your joy in achieving new things and also share your child's joy in their own achievements. Think of yourself as a part of the learning team, and your child as just as important a part of the team as you. Give them kudos, clap for them, tell friends and relatives about their achievements, and post their work, awards or photos of their activities as you would for a toddler.

At elementary age, your child can benefit from gymnastics, dance, or music lessons even if they did not start when they were younger. They can enjoy theater troupes, group sports or lessons in tennis or golf. Take a look at your community's calendar of events in the newspaper or online and go through it with your child to help them choose activities they would like to be involved in after school or during the summer.

Even though your child has already explored many different types of activities, keep sharing new types experiences with them. At the elementary age, your child is ready to learn more details and refine their abilities. Allow your child to set

43

their own expectations for success, and always keep up your enthusiasm. Your child is counting on you to help them master their world in their own special way. Your role is to be a facilitator of learning, a teacher, and a cheering section. You can point out things that make you happy and proud, but it is not your role to criticize their progress. Be positive and supportive as your child develops their strengths into bona fide talents.

Tips for Maximizing Talent Development

Aside from specific learning activities for developing each type of talent, there are also steps you can take to make the most of your child's days. Providing basic structure in their lives is important, especially when they are toddlers through elementary age. In addition you can create inspirational moments that stay with your child throughout their childhood and as they keep developing their talents into their adulthood.

Schedule Activities

Schedules are important in the lives of toddlers. Try to set up times for each activity your child does each day. For example, you might have music activities at 2 p.m., naptime at 3 p.m., exercise play at 4 p.m., free time at 5 p.m. and dinner at 7 p.m. Whatever schedule works best for you and allows your child opportunities to explore their world is best. The schedule does not have to be rigid – change it when you need to or when your child is excited about doing a different activity than the one you have planned. However, try to keep to the schedule as much as possible to give your child a sense of security as well as definite experiences to look forward to later in the day.

Provide Live Exposure to Talented People

Watching talented people perform in real life can have a major impact in shaping your child's dreams and ambitions. If your child is interested in playing the piano, take them to see a concert pianist. Your child can get inspiration from seeing great singers or talented actors perform on stage. If your child is interested in a sport, take them to a professional or college level baseball, football, hockey or soccer game, or take them to a tennis match or a golf tournament.

Refrain from comparing your child's achievements to the talents of a great performer, athlete, writer or artist. Let your child make the connection between what they are working at and what the talented person has achieved. Instead of pointing out how much they will have to work to get to where this gifted person has arrived in their career, focus on the rewards they enjoy for living out their dreams.

Take the contact with talented individuals a step further by introducing your child to talented people directly. You can ask these local or national stars to visit your child's school for an assembly. Or, you can create one-on-one experiences by introducing your child to your most talented acquaintances. Bring your child to the sports arena or playing field to meet athletes in person when the team has a children's day. Never assume that a talented person does not have time to spend a few moments with your child. Many local and national celebrities actually enjoy encouraging young children to reach for the success that these talented people have already achieved.

Wrapping Up

Childhood is the best time to encourage a playful and joyful approach to learning. During the toddler and elementary ages, your child can explore talent areas based on their strengths and then refine their talents. You can facilitate this by making learning toys, games and materials for them to explore and learn to use. You can help them learn by offering gentle and joyful guidance. You can put extra effort into giving them the best opportunities for learning. Yet you do not have to buy art supplies, activity sets or send them to classes to help them learn. They can learn from everyday experiences, right in their own home and community.

CHAPTER 4

HOW TO TURN EVERYDAY EVENTS
INTO LEARNING OPPORTUNITIES

As an adult, you show your skills and talents as you go about your everyday life. When your children are young, they need to learn life skills too. While they are learning these basic life skills, you can also encourage them to learn about the greater implications and possibilities of having these skills and talents. Use the everyday activities that are already happening in your home and community to present new opportunities for learning and developing their personal strengths.

Opportunities to Learn about Important Skills and Personal Qualities

Your child needs a chance to grow up in an environment where learning is an everyday part of life. Developing your child's inner strengths can help them be self sufficient later on in life and give them a boost toward a profitable career. Don't push career goals at this age. Just focus on helping your child develop their skills and personal qualities that you know are crucial to your child's success in life.

Kindness

Children sometimes seem predisposed to showing kindness to others. Yet kindness is at least partly a learned skill. This is an important strength to develop, and it is one that will improve their lives and the lives of those around them. Show your kindness to your child as a toddler exploring their world or as an elementary child refining their talents.

You can also encourage them to show kindness to their playmates and members of the family and praise them for doing so. As you go about your day, take every opportunity to help others and show them that you care about them.

Get involved with the life of your community by helping with volunteer activities. Whenever possible, allow your children to come with you and help. Model an attitude of caring and compassion without unnecessary judgments and criticisms. Show your child it is a good thing to offer kindness to others.

Always remember that, if you are a good and loving parent, your child wants to be like you.

Friendliness

Having excellent social skills can not only make your children feel better about themselves, but it can also improve their chances for success later on in their chosen career. Teach your children to interact with your family members and friends in a positive way. Show them how to start conversations and praise them when they bring up an interesting topic.

Common courtesy is a crucial part of being friendly, too. Always say hello, good- bye, good morning and good night to acknowledge the presence and departure of each family member. Do not let people come and go without saying something friendly. Say please, thank you and excuse me, and encourage your child to do the same.

One of the keys to developing more advanced social skills is learning how to reach out to people who are shy or uncomfortable in social situations. When you meet someone like this or invite them into your home, show your child that it is okay to talk to someone without the other person making the first move. Show them how to gently include this shy person in a conversation and draw out the person's natural personality.

50

Sensitivity

A child who is overly sensitive can live a very hard life, especially if this sensitivity finds expression in their emotions. However, even an extremely emotional child offers something valuable to the world through their highly developed sensitivity to the world around them.

Find out what your child is sensitive to, and help them find ways to express their sensitivity without feeling overwhelmed. If your child is sensitive to the feelings of others, talk to them about positive ways to express those feelings. If your child is sensitive to visual images, place strict limits on media viewing and steer them toward expression through art or photography.

Children who are sensitive to noises often shy away from loud music. It seems to overwhelm their senses. Yet you can still develop this sensitivity by guiding your child toward activities like listening to quieter music, playing an instrument softly or listening to poetry as you read. Your child's sensitivity can sometimes seem unbearable to them. Your job is to tone it down enough for your child to recognize the value of seeing, hearing and understanding things in a more vivid way than others.

Sense of Humor

A great sense of humor can take your child far in life. People enjoy spending time with others who are humorous, whether at play, during activities, at school or even at work. If your child has a very highly developed sense of humor, they might even go on to be a comedian, a comic actor or a comedy writer. So, developing their sense of humor early can be a very positive thing.

How do you encourage your child to develop a sense of humor? First, have a sense of humor yourself. If you have never thought of yourself as funny, do not try to be a comedian now. However, you can look for gentle humor in everyday occurrences. Avoid trying to be funny when someone is injured, although you can help them see the lighter side of the situation.

Then, encourage your child's attempts at humor. When they draw a picture or tell a story, notice if they are smiling in a silly way or even laughing. Join in their spirit of fun. You don't have to laugh at things that are not funny to you. Yet if you think that other good people would find it funny, you can still comment that your child just did or said a funny thing. Avoid sarcasm and focus on positive humor.

Patience

Pay attention to the way your child approaches tasks. Do they keep working even if the task is difficult for them? Do they keep trying different solutions until they find one that works? If your child seems to be struggling or feeling frustrated, praise them for their patience so far. Tell them, "I know you can do it!"

One mistake many parents make is to rescue their child when they are having a hard time completing a task or project. They reason that the task or project must be done regardless of who does it. In some cases, this is true. But usually, your child will gain a better benefit and develop their level of patience by keeping at it themselves until they solve the problem or complete the task to their own satisfaction.

When you see the finished result of the child's hard work, congratulate them on their willingness to keep trying. If you don't like the results, I suggest one of two options. Either focus on the child's gift for patience and let the child be happy about meeting their own expectations. Or, if it is something that must be done a certain way, you can work with them further as they finish or correct the task. Try to always let your child finish the job if it is within their capabilities.

Attention Span

Attention span is one part of patience that is very important to develop. Keep your child engaged in learning activities as long as possible, or until your child begins to lose interest. You have to give them sustained attention before you can expect them to be attentive.

Teach them how to minimize or ignore distractions. For example, you can help your child develop the habit of turning off media while they are involved in a complex task. For a time, multitasking was the buzzword for productivity. Newer research shows that trying to do several tasks at once can keep you from doing any of them well. Teach your child to focus on one activity at a time, to learn one skill at a time or to work on developing one talent at a time. They can mix it up throughout the day, but each moment needs to be focused on one task.

A complex task can seem overwhelming to a child, and what seems complex depends on their age and stage of development. To increase their concentration on the larger challenges, break them down into smaller steps or tasks. Celebrate when your child completes each task along the way, and encourage them to go on to the next task after you celebrate.

Elementary children are put in a class, sometimes a large class, all day during school. There is very little one-to-one interaction with teachers in most schools. Sometimes all these school children need is special individual attention from you when they get home. Spend the time working with your child on developing their strengths into talents.

Exercise can also help your child pay attention. Keep the exercises simple for toddlers. Put on music and dance or do movements to the melodies and words. Elementary children can take a break from learning after school to ride a bike, play an active game, or take a short swim.

Restrict on time spent viewing TV or other passive media. Keep your child involved and mentally or physically active during the day. Even when you read bedtime stories at night, involve your child by asking fun questions about the story or the pictures in a child's book.

Take care of your child's needs that can disrupt their attention span. If their focus flags, find out if they are hungry, thirsty or uncomfortable with the temperature in your home. Solve all these problems before you expect your child to stay focused on a task or activity. Then, teach your child to recognize and take care of these needs for themselves.

Financial Adeptness

Is your child good at counting and identifying money? Do they have an interest in financial matters? Are they interested in the future financial success of your family? If so, encourage these interests and talents. A financially adept child can grow into a financially strong adult. They can manage their own or their family's money well in any case; and if they are very gifted and very interested, they might go into some financial career field.

You can start teaching your child about saving as soon as they can pick up a coin and put it into a piggy bank instead of into their mouths. When they get a little older, they can start to understand the real value of saving. Ask your 4-5 year old toddler what they would like to have, and tell them that they can save the money to buy it. Do not state this as a harsh expectation. Instead, make it something fun and rewarding to do. Take the money out of the piggy bank once a week or even once a month, and count it with your child counting along. Then, let them know how much more they need to save to get what they want to buy.

When your child has saved enough, make it a point to go out with them immediately to get it, or order it online the day they have reached their goal.

As your child gets a little older and handling coins and bills becomes second nature, focus more on the concept of saving for important goals. One way to proceed is to have three piggy banks or money boxes for them to save in.

Encourage them to put into each of the three banks equal amounts of the money they receive as gifts, rewards, tokens of affection or coins they find while doing simple cleaning chores. The first is for anytime money, the second is for a small goal, and the third is for long-term savings.

Your elementary child is old enough to start thinking of saving for life goals like getting a car, going to college, or renting their first apartment. That one long-term piggy bank can be a great asset when your child gets older. They have a long time to save and that money just keeps adding up year after year. Since they have the other two containers to save for immediate and small goals, you can satisfy their needs for experiencing the rewards of saving right now.

Introduce your older elementary child to the concept of budgeting. Help them learn to identify their personal needs and figure out how much money you and they can contribute toward meeting those needs. Continue to work with them on refining their budget by including more things they need and eliminating unnecessary expenses. This exercise can translate into business acumen later in life.

Mechanical Aptitude

Mechanical aptitude is the innate ability to look and tinker with toys and later machines to fix them, improve them or put them together. Everyone needs some mechanical skills to take them through everyday life. For example, if you have never driven a new car before, you need the skill to figure out how to open the trunk and turn on the windshield wipers. You can teach young children how to do these simple mechanical tasks easily.

When your child is a toddler, you can offer them toy sets that are made to be put together and taken apart. If your child seems to have a gift for doing mechanical tasks during elementary school, you can offer them small appliances that no longer work to experiment with and develop their mechanical skills even further. As older elementary children, they can even help you fix something major. You can encourage them to examine the items you are fixing or assembling and ask them for suggestions on what to do next. These skills help them in daily life, and can result in a lifetime career in working on or designing cars, trains or airplanes, or choose another life path that uses these mechanical skills.

Planning Skills

Everyone fares better in life if they have some skill in planning. Children who show special aptitude for planning the everyday events in their life benefit greatly from developing these skills. A child who is good at planning things can later find success in career fields like business, design, teaching, being a community or wedding planner, or orchestrating large local or even national events.

Start by giving your toddler the chance to say what they would like to do first when you create or change their daily schedule. When they get into elementary school, let them help plan a meal for the next day. They can choose the foods they want to have at a meal, and you can let them check the cabinets or refrigerator to see if you already have what you need to make the meal. Then, ask them what things you didn't have that you need to add to your shopping list and take them along with you when you go. Cook the meal and tell other family members and friends that the child helped you plan the meal.

Include your child in family vacation plans. Show them your brochures or online photos of the vacation destination and ask them which sights they would like to see, what activities they want to try, and what events they would like to attend. As they get closer to the end of their elementary school, you can even give them one day of the vacation to plan on their own. Guide them to choose things they and others in the family can enjoy.

Another opportunity for learning about planning is to allow your child to help in plans for a birthday party, a family outing or a holiday celebration. Listen to their ideas and consider them seriously. Incorporate at least one, and preferably several, into your plans for the special day.

Skills at Taking Care of Animals

If you have family pets or a family farm, encourage your child to interact with animals on a daily basis. They can help feed, and water the animals and do simple grooming tasks. As they get older, you can teach them how to do simple caretaking tasks when the pet is injured or ill. A child who is good with animals can later find enjoyment and companionship by having a pet. If they have the aptitude and spend significant time developing it, they can go on to become a veterinarian or a successful dairy farmer or rancher.

Gardening Skills

Many children like working in the garden with their parents and grandparents. Nurture this interest by giving your child more opportunities to take care of plants. Give them seeds to plant their own vegetables or flowers. Explain how often they need to be watered and tended, and let the child take care of them. Give them gentle reminders to tend to their plants, but never criticize or show anger with them for neglecting their plant or letting it die. Instead, ask the child what they could have done differently and encourage them to try again. A child who is gifted at gardening can later become a crop farmer, a flower shop owner or an agricultural scientist.

Cooking Skills

Most children love to cook, and some children excel at it. Involve your child to help you prepare desserts, snacks and meals. When they are 3 and older, they can do small cooking tasks like adding cups of flour or sugar, pouring in milk or oil, and greasing a pan. By the time they are 4 or 5, they can begin stirring and gathering ingredients, and cutting out sugar cookies or biscuits. When they get into early elementary, they can measure ingredients and decorate cookies. At later elementary age, they can begin to read and follow recipes, knead dough, and even prepare entire simple meals. Encourage your child to cook and participate as you prepare foods. A child who loves and excels at cooking can become a chef, a nutritionist or a restaurateur. In addition, the skills of measuring and following directions learned in the kitchen can help your child become a scientist.

Aptitude for Logical Thought

If your child seems to reason out everything using logical reasoning, they might have a special aptitude that can serve them in virtually any career field, most notably computer career fields. Encourage logical thought by prompting your child to think about the reasons for everyday occurrences in your home. Young elementary children can try simple puzzle books and then move on to more complicated ones. As they get older, they can begin to do advanced logic puzzles and reason out more complex issues.

As you go about your daily life, keep hold of the idea that every situation is an opportunity to teach your child something or encourage them to learn on their own. Offer ideas and gentle guidance to help them make the most of these early years. Then, when they accomplish something meaningful, no matter how small, you can help them appreciate their success with a happy celebration.

CHAPTER 5

CELEBRATE ACHIEVEMENTS, NO MATTER HOW SMALL

Celebrations are an important part of learning and becoming. When you celebrate with your child, you give them the gift of appreciating them for who they are and for what they have done. You help them connect joy and other positive emotions with accomplishment and development. You help them enjoy the everyday pleasures of learning new things. It doesn't matter whether the achievement is a small one or a major one. As long as they have successfully learned a valuable skill, it is worth celebrating. Match the level of celebration with the effort involved or the level of achievement. This is how your child learns to reach for the stars but enjoy every step along the way.

Expressing Appreciation

The simplest celebrations are also some of the most effective ones. You can do them every day when your child creates something or succeeds at some new, small task. You can also do them when your child does something phenomenal or completes a long-term goal like graduating from kindergarten or elementary school.

What are these small celebrations? They are based on expressing joy, pride and appreciation for the child's achievements. Smile when your child learns something new. Proudly show off their creations. Clap for them when they try a new gymnastic or dance move, or when they play an instrument for you.

Telling Others of Your Child's Successes

Sharing your child's successes can be a kind of small celebration in itself. When your toddler or elementary child does something new, advances a skill or develops a talent, offer them the chance to call a beloved relative to tell them about the achievement. Calling grandma, grandpa, or their favorite aunt or uncle can brighten their day and heighten their joy in learning.

It is also a form of celebration when you announce your child's accomplishments to others. It is important to praise your child directly. However, when you tell someone else, your child gets an even better sense of your appreciation of their success.

Offering Rewards

It is usually a mistake to hold a carrot out to a child to encourage achievement. It is much better to help your child develop an intrinsic motivation for learning. Offer a reward after the child has completed the accomplishment. Have special rewards ready to hand out after your child does something new or special. The rewards can be simple, but avoid making junk food and desserts the standard reward. They can be fun occasionally, but you do not want your child to associate accomplishment with unhealthy habits. Mix things up with rewards as diverse as toys, puzzle or coloring books, and videos or music time complete with noisemakers and confetti.

Spur-of-the-Moment Celebrations

When your child accomplishes something unexpected, it is fun and exciting to think of a way to celebrate in that moment. You can take a trip to the ice cream store for a treat, take your child out to shop for new clothing or toys, or invite over your child's best friend for a cookout. Make sure the reward is something your child can enjoy. If you are not sure what can make your child happy in that moment, simply ask them for suggestions.

Quiet Celebrations

If your child is very sensitive or quiet, they might prefer a quiet, leisurely celebration. Go to the park alone with them and enjoy nature and a friendly chat. Listen to soft music and give and receive hugs. Play a board game with them.

Give them your special attention and spend quality time with them.

Celebrating After Their Activity Performances

Music, gymnastic, sports, theater or other performance activities deserve special recognition on performance day. Attend every performance possible, pay attention, and cheer your child on from the audience. When the show is over, give your young child a flower to wear. Shower them with affection and show your pride. Avoid stealing their spotlight, though. Performance days are not about you and your excellent parenting skills. Instead, they are all about celebrating your child's newly refined skills, talents and ambitions.

Family Celebrations

Celebrating each family member's success with a family celebration encourages an atmosphere of teamwork and mutual respect. Do not be the parent that sees respect as something reserved for adults. Instead, learn to respect your children for making good choices, learning new things, developing valuable personal qualities, creating something new or performing well.

Going out to a movie, restaurant or recreation center together is a good reward. Even easier is a celebration right in your own home. Get the family together and have a fun day in the backyard. Celebrate a toddler's accomplishments with a family bubble-blowing festival or a game of tag. Let the elementary child who is celebrating an achievement choose an activity like kickball, croquet, volleyball or badminton.

Celebrations with Friends

Children love to celebrate special events with their friends. So, why not give your child the opportunity to share their successes with their playmates and friends? Treat everyone to a special play date or outing. If the celebration is for creating or building something new, use that item as a centerpiece on the table during snack time. If you want to celebrate your child's performance, take their friends along with you to the event. When it is over, you can all spend some fun time together on the way home or after you arrive there.

Celebrating Major Accomplishments

You definitely need to plan very special celebrations for your child's most important achievements. Failing to acknowledge your child's major accomplishments can have a devastating effect on their self esteem.

The first thing you need to do is to know or find out what the biggest accomplishments are for any skill or expression of talent in each type of activity in which your child participates. Are there exceptional feats of athletic prowess your child should be congratulated for in a sport? Ask their coach if you don't know already. Did your child excel in a gymnastics competition or a music contest? Again, just ask the person in charge. When your child has a major milestone coming up like a graduation or receiving an award, mark the date on your calendar and, whatever you do, don't let the date go by without acknowledging the effort your child has put into making it a success.

Next, you need to plan a great celebration for the achievement. Invite members of your extended family or family friends to come over and join in the party. Have cake and punch. Or, choose healthier options like unsalted nuts, a veggie tray with fat-free dip, and juice or sparkling cider. Put up decorations and a banner to create a festive atmosphere. Choose upbeat music and create the soundtrack for the event. During the event, take a moment to stand up in front of all and explain the accomplishment. Tell everyone how proud you are and congratulate your child.

Keeping Up an Attitude of Celebration

Celebrations are not just for specific achievements. You can create a more positive environment for learning by keeping up an attitude of celebration every day. Celebrate your child's innate abilities and talents. Celebrate your child's personal victories and when they accomplish something that is important only to them. Celebrate the joy your child brings into your world. In short, celebrate life!

CONCLUSION

Children start developing their strengths with or without your guidance. It is a natural part of growing. Yet your child has very little chance of reaching their fullest potential on their own. As a parent, give your child the love and understanding they need to learn new things and develop strengths into talents.

Learn the best ways to teach your child and provide learning opportunities without pushing them into something they do not want to do or are not ready to do. Your child can develop at their own rate and still accomplish great things. Be sensitive to your child's responses to learning activities and encourage them to express their emotions. Think positively in every instance.

As you work with your child during the toddler and elementary years, give them your full support when they are trying to achieve something. Then, when they succeed, take time to celebrate their accomplishments. Your child can develop a love of learning along with the skills they learn and talents they develop. You can be the right kind of parent to help your child be the best they can be!

Printed by Libri Plureos GmbH in Hamburg, Germany